Lingualism –
How Nations Compete For
Terminologies

BOOKS BY THORSTEN PATTBERG

The East-West Dichotomy

Shengren

Inside Peking University

Language Imperialism

Corruption in China

Diary of a Mad Imperialist

The Euro-Tao

Lingualism

Press Soldiers

Knowledge is a Polyglot

LINGUALISM – How Nations Compete For Terminologies

A New Frontier In Culture Studies

THORSTEN PATTBERG

ISBN: 0-9842091-5-8
ISBN-13: 978-0-9842091-5-6

**lod
press
new
york**

Printed in the United States

For Gu Zhengkun
and Duan Qing
In Friendship

INTRODUCTION

Dr. Pattberg brought back the "shengren" to two billion East-Asians, and is the leader of a Confucian movement in Europe. He has published widely on Language Imperialism, the End of Translation, and the Future of Global Language. His efforts have now culminated in LINGUALISM, the bold proposal that asks nations to compete for their terminologies just like they compete for everything else in the world. This is a game-changing text: culturally significant, highly provocative, and, above all, globally relevant.

LINGUALISM – HOW NATIONS COMPETE FOR TERMINOLOGIES

"The limits of my language mean the limits of my world." - Ludwig Wittgenstein

Capitalism forces people to compete for market shares, natural resources, and human capital. Less obviously so, they must also compete for terminologies. I call this *lingualism*.

"Philosophy," "religion," and "science" are ideological concepts that serve the needs of the dominant West, and, in the past, were hardly ever challenged. In this century, however, this could change, by means of calling into question an archaic and fallible model of knowledge acquisition: translation.

Due to the one-time European conquest of the world, most of those who became European subjects took in European vocabularies, with the result that the vast majority of students no longer had any other terminologies available to them other than philosophy, religion, and science to categorize the whole range of human thought.

This reduction of all the world's vocabularies to a set of inherently European words made it effortless for our elites to, for example, compose a *Philosophy of China* without using a single original Chinese term.

In the West we believe the word "philosophy" includes all non-European thought, while knowing it is firmly rooted in the Greco-Hellenic tradition. We paradoxically treat it as universal to others and unique to us at the same time. Thus, a book entitled *History of Philosophy* may include a chapter on Confucius, or it may not; either way it would not fail to fulfill its title's promise.

If you asked an American, "What is the world's *greatest* syndicate?" you would probably get an answer such as that it's the trade unions, the corporate media, the Freemasons, or maybe the anarchists. Actually, it's none of these—it's the philosophers.

Looking a little bit closer at written history, we can see that "philosopher" wasn't even a concept in East Asia before Nishi Amane translated it into the Japanese term *tetsugakusha* around 1871. There is no instance of the word "philosophy" (now expressed in Chinese as *zhexue*) appearing in any of the East Asian classics. Therefore, our books on "Chinese Philosophy" are distortions of the original, as are our "Departments of Eastern Philosophy."

What started in Greece as Plato's school of philosophy (the *Akademia*) eliminated all its competitors and has now become some sort of compulsory membership scheme for all of the world's thinkers. No top scholar shall leave our universities without a PhD—a "Doctor of Philosophy"—even if their subject of study has nothing to do with philosophy.

As any reputable linguist can tell you, the vocabularies of the world's languages add up, they don't overlap. Translation always amounts to reduction: one word acknowledged, another … eliminated.

Via this process of destruction of foreign words, we've laid our hands on the Chinese *shengren* —and *seijin* in Japanese, and *seong-in* in Korean—and altered, or, as the official term goes, "translated" them as "Chinese philosophers," "Japanese philosophers," and "Korean philosophers." And we have, metaphorically speaking, demolished China's spiritual *wenming* and Japan's *bunmei*, which we now re-imagine, in our European fashion, as materialistic "civilizations." Thousands of scholars, all Doctors of Philosophy, endeavor to make such "corrections" to human knowledge look like the original. The public is unable to tell the difference between a *shengren* and a philosopher; they cannot know what has been omitted from their textbooks.

In fact, Confucius was a *shengren*. A *shengren* is the highest member in the family-based Chinese values tradition, a sage that has the highest moral standards, called *de*, who applies the principles of *ren*, *li*, *yi*, *zhi* and *xin* (and 10 more), and connects with all people as if they were his family. Few people in the West, even among the most educated, have ever heard of a *shengren*, simply because this word has been omitted and willfully replaced by a convenient translation.

Now consider "religion." Religion is Christianity. Whether we consent to it or not, we all live in the year 2013 A.D., the Year of Our Lord Jesus Christ. By labeling teachings like Buddhism or Confucianism as "religion," we can pull our own Religion over them, and administer them in our books on "World Religions." Could you imagine the President of the United States saying: "Allah Bless America!"? Would the Pope call Jesus Christ or St. Nikolas a "buddha," or a "shengren"? No. Yet we insist, at all times, that Muslims pray to God; that Confucius was a philosopher.

Western students are taught that there arc "saints" and "philosophers" all over Asia, yet evidently there isn't a single *shengren*, *buddha*, or *bodhisattva* in Europe or America. Today, few

Westerners are able to distinguish between, say, a *rabbi*, a *guru*, a *heshang*, an *ulama*, and a *junzi*. Instead, in most Western schools those concepts are all steamrolled by a single convenient translation: the "priest."

The West exported all its historical revelations like the Resurrection, the Enlightenment, and Colonialism, and established virtually all academic disciplines— even the very concept of "university," a Greek concept. Who's ever heard of *guoxue*, a distinct Chinese academic discipline dedicated to the study of ancient Chinese culture and civilization? Or of *daxue*, the Confucian way of highest learning?

Perhaps our greatest invention yet was "science." Maybe equally admirable ideas exist in India's vast realms of *shastras* and *sutras*, or in the Persian realms of *elm* and *hekmat*, or still exist in countless Chinese teachings. Yet, people are taught it is "science"—a Western word and concept—that we all should aspire to: Science. When the European scientists "discovered" foreign lands, they swept away local knowledge (often accumulated over hundreds of years) and chose their own imported or newly-invented terminologies and classifications over those of the indigenous people—as if indigenous knowledge didn't exist.

In addition, the West provided all classifications and labels in the natural and life sciences. Think about European names—mostly from Latin or Greek—in chemistry, biology, and zoology. Mythical creatures that exist solely in China like the *long* or the *qilin* are reinvented by affixing the adjective "Chinese" to a Western semantic: the "Chinese dragon" and the "Chinese unicorn." And even a living creature unique to China, the *xiongmao*, a giant carnivore whose diet is 99% bamboo and who is found primarily in Sichuan province, isn't known in the West by its Chinese name. We call it a "panda."

People tend to forget that dictionaries and nation states with language policies aren't natural. They are artificial things, man-made institutions that people as limited as you and I thought up to describe *everything*. Think of a Dutch dictionary whose authors were determined to contain the world's entire knowledge(s), ideas, and thoughts—past, present, and future. For centuries, such European scholars were "discovering" unique foreign cultures and dispossessing them: "What is this, *dharma*? Ok, let's call it 'law'," or "What is that, *daode*? Ok, let's call it 'virtue'." We might as well conclude that most translators work for nationhood, not for knowledge. They are *destroyers*, not protectors, of foreign knowledge.

Globalization is often a brilliant euphemism for this destruction of non-Western ideas. We want "economy," not *jingji*. We want "politics," not *zhengzhi*. For us to be able to grasp all the nuances, forms, paradigms, experience, and history of a Chinese concept such as *tianxia* (literally, "under heaven"), Western scholars would effectively have to *become* Chinese—i.e., to sinicize themselves. This is not going to happen. In fact, the exact opposite is the case: the Chinese (and all other Eastern) people need to learn and grasp Western concepts. They have to westernize themselves.

We demand "democracy" and "human rights" in China, yet technically these words don't exist there. Yes, the Chinese may adopt those Western concepts, but imagine if China today were to demand from the West to foster *datong* and become a proper *wenming*. Translations of these terms would give us nothing here: "great community" and "civilization." We would be clueless as to what China wants of us. Why? Because we don't have those concepts in the West, and no translation can ever bring them. The only way to understand *datong* and *wenming* (and any other non-Western concept) is to learn it, and through that acknowledge its existence.

But foreign concepts like *daxue*, *shengren*, or *junzi* have unorthodox meanings; in the West, they are unwanted thought. Europe has a history of anxiety of having too much contact with foreign thought. In 1677, Gottfried Wilhelm Leibniz, the first German philosopher, advised his countrymen to avoid "foreign or Unteutsch words," of which "the biggest question existeth whether to tolerate them at all." In 1921, Nobel laureate Hermann Hesse cautioned that "We cannot and we must not become Chinese, and at heart we don't want to either." Anxiety over cultural differences could be seen in Edmund Husserl's remark in 1935 that something was unique about Europe and that "if we understand ourselves properly, we would never indianize ourselves, for example."

German students learn foreign languages such as Sanskrit, Hindi, Chinese, Japanese, and Arabic using an artificial go-between-language, like the infamous *pinyin* in Chinese—a system using Western writing characters which is now used by all mainland Chinese. Instead of learning the target foreign writing system such as devanagari, hiragana, or hanzi, they start with its *romanization* (literally: "to make Roman"), which is simply a transliteration of the foreign alphabet into Roman letters. This then forever prevents the students from learning foreign languages like the natives do. Even if they wanted "to become indianized" (in Husserl's words), they could not do so.

Yes, all cultures export *some* of their ideas and concepts. In comparison, however, the East Asians keep their socio-cultural originality largely to themselves. It is often said that due to Western imperialism and colonialism, the Eastern hemisphere has too much respect for the Western powers. Chinese students are eagerly studying, and often imitating the West. The same is true with Japanese students. But the Western understanding of East Asia is still a murky confusion. Ask a group of Western students, "When is the Chinese New Year?" Or, "What year is it in Japan?" They will most likely reply: "It's January 1st." Or, "It's the year 2013 A.D., of course." The correct answers are: February 10th of *Shenian*, the Year of the Snake, and *Heisei* 25 *Nen*, the 25th year of the current emperor's reign.

How can we end translation in cases where it serves us no good or even eliminates knowledge? Or better yet: what can we do for the future of global language? The answer to this is easier than you might think. I firmly believe that the only way to a truly global language is the adoption of many more Chinese (and other foreign) key terminologies into our reports and writings. People are born curious, and when they see a word like *shengren* that they don't know, they will study it and learn it. They won't learn anything new if we just give them another "Chinese saint."

The European missionaries and philosophers have plastered the entire global scholarship with their complacent European translations of non-European ideas, and it will take time to fix this. But will we do this? My personal experience from Western academia is that it will never allow foreign terminology— with Eastern shades of meaning—to weaken our *lingualism*. We call things the way we want, and we call this "freedom."

And our version of "freedom" shall trump all others.

ABOUT THE AUTHOR

Dr. Thorsten Pattberg (裴德思) is a German philosopher and cultural critic.

He attended Edinburgh University, Fudan University, Tokyo University and Harvard University, and earned his doctorate degree from The Institute of World Literature at Peking University.

Dr. Pattberg is a former Research Fellow at the Institute for Advanced Humanistic Studies at Peking University, and former Foreign Research Fellow at Tokyo University.

Lingualism was first published in 'Asia, Pacific, World', a Berghahn journal, in 2013.

The views expressed in this work are solely those of the author and do not necessarily reflect the views or policies of the above-mentioned institutions.

THORSTEN PATTBERG

LINGUALISM